Daddy's Beard + Super Daddy

Published by BnMs Empire LTD

bnmsempire@gmail.com

www.comestudywithme.com

© BnMs Empire LTD 2017

BnMs Empire LTD

All rights reserved. Without limiting the rights under copyright reserved above, no part of this publication may be reproduced, stored in or introduced into a retrieval system, or transmitted in any form or by any form or by any means (electronic, mechanical, photocopying, recording or otherwise), without the prior written permission of both the copyright owner and the above publisher of this book.

A catalogue record of this book is available from the British Library.

ISBN: 978-1-9998912-1-3

For Malachi and Biel

Kindly edited by Pauline E Reynolds

This book belongs to ……………………………………………..

From……………………………………………………………………..

Daddy's Beard

When he rubs his beard on my little face, it feels spiky and prickly making me move away quickly.

Even though it's rough and hard, I like it really because it makes me all tickly.

When I pull on his beard hard, he shouts "Ouch".

I then move fast and cling to the couch.

Loud noise is scary but his beard is hairy. Even though he makes me jump, I don't ever get in a grump.

No one is as funny as my daddy. When he holds me up and tickles my tummy.

Super Daddy

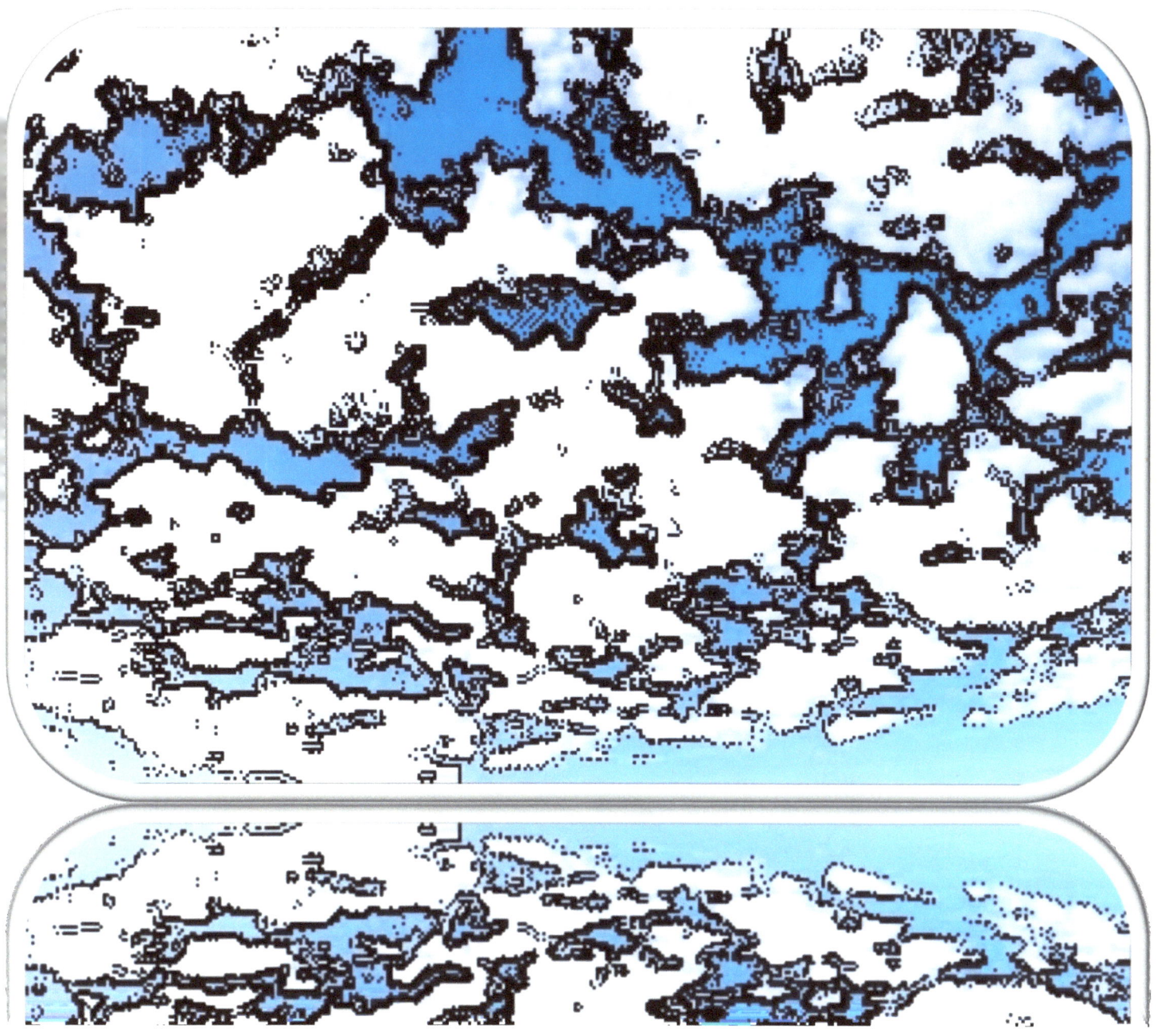

When I fly around and around, I don't ever want to reach the ground.

Daddy why are you so big and strong?

You always hold me up for so long.

Sometimes you sneak up behind me and give me a fright.

So I hold on to you very very tight.

But when I realise it is you holding me dad, I loosen my grip because I feel so glad.

Being a super dad isn't just about games and being funny. When we're all sick, out he comes with ginger, lemon and honey.

He will do anything to help us stay strong and healthy.

Milangu Community School was built in 2015. Previously, there were no schools in the Milangu area, leaving the children of the area without an option for an education. With the help from volunteers and friends from all over the word a three classroom primary school and boys/girls toilet houses was built. One of the classrooms serves as an Early Childhood Development centre and Work Skills Training Centre for the local women. The plan is to teach the local women work skills that will allow them to bring in income that will benefit their families and a percentage of it will go to supporting the costs of running the new school (food for the children, pay for teachers). The new primary school has ~70 children enrolled and started classes the first week of July 2016. The children and the school were provided with school supplies, such as children's books, chalk, pencils , and crayons funded by volunteers,

The school is 100% run by volunteers and food for the children is grown on site in the schools garden.

Please support our wonderful school in Zambia by sharing our books with others. 10p from the sale of every book will go towards the maintenance of this fantastic school.

If you would like hands on experience working in the school in Zambia, please email bnmsempire@gmail.com who will pass your details to the organiser.

www.ingramcontent.com/pod-product-compliance
Lightning Source LLC
Chambersburg PA
CBHW041233040426
42444CB00002B/141